To Evelyn
I Hope you get as
much out of this prayer
Book as I have.
I love to read it each
night. I got one.
for myself as well.
           all my love
Well done Evelyn
one day at a time.
              Marie.
          X X X X
           X X X X X

PRAYER AT NIGHT'S APPROACHING

❖❖❖❖❖❖❖❖❖❖❖❖❖

JIM COTTER

CAIRNS PUBLICATIONS

SHEFFIELD

in association with

ARTHUR JAMES

BERKHAMSTED

1997

© Copyright by Jim Cotter,
1983, 1991, 1997

First published 1983,
the first four editions with the title *Prayer at Night*
Fifth edition 1997

CAIRNS PUBLICATIONS
47 Firth Park Avenue
Sheffield
S5 6HF

ARTHUR JAMES LTD
70 Cross Oak Road
Berkhamsted
Hertfordshire
HP4 3HZ

Further copies of this book and other Cairns Publications
can be obtained from Arthur James Ltd

ISBN 0 85305 419 3

Typeset in Monotype Baskerville
by Strathmore Publishing Services, London N7

Printed by Biddles Ltd, Guildford

CONTENTS

WITH GRATITUDE
to those who have helped me to take a few steps
on the way of God's Love,
and in particular to those
who have encouraged and assisted me
in the compiling of Prayer at Night:

JANE of Fairacres, Oxford,
now of fairer acres still

NADIR of Jersey

ESTHER of Canterbury,
now of Rowlestone in Herefordshire

RYDER of London

PREFACE

'I like the larger print, but the book won't fit in my handbag.' 'I like the pocket size, but my eyes object to the small print.' These comments, backed up by encouragement from my new associates at Arthur James Ltd, have led me to compile this fifth edition of *Prayer at Night* in one format only, pocket size but 11 point type. Since it was first published fifteen years ago, the book has sold twenty thousand copies, and I have been moved by the letters of appreciation sent to me. I should like the dedication on the opposite page to include those unnamed correspondents as well as the named friends who first encouraged me.

So this book has played a significant role in my life. Like most important things it was triggered by an incident which in itself carried no hint of what was to happen. I had been praying the ancient late evening service of Compline in a version in modern English. It occurred to me that I had addressed God as 'Lord' rather frequently in no more than ten minutes. I did a count and the total was thirty-six. 'Father' came second with twelve. All the other biblical images for God were either omitted or rarely used.

At the time I was beginning to realize that the prayer of the Christian Church had been slanted by a patriarchy and hierarchy of men who took nearly all the decisions and held nearly all the power. Rather than merely criticize, I was galvanized into attempting a variant. So *Prayer at Night* was born, with the intention of using a greater variety of both picture language and overall material than does the traditional order, yet keeping the same basic structure.

Some find the more official modern language versions of Compline simple and austere, others find them repetitive and threadbare. For the latter, *Prayer at Night* seems to have struck a chord and enabled them to keep on praying. One correspondent wrote that she could use the book at the end of a heavy day when her brain was hurting.

I hope this new edition will continue to prove helpful both at the end of the day and during the night, in hours of sleeplessness or vigil. Those familiar with the previous editions will notice quite a few changes. Doubtless these will be improvements to some, irritations to others! But by bringing together all the material needed for any one night of the week, rather than distributing it in sections, I at least intend to make the book less fussy to use. It should also be easy to mark the page where provision is made for readings and antiphons (short

prayers before the Nunc Dimittis, the outburst of
praise by old Simeon in the story of the Presen-
tation of Jesus in the Temple in Jerusalem) for
special days and seasons. There are a couple of
blank pages for each day of the week for your own
particular prayers. And there is a kind of appendix
of additional prayers which draws on material from
previous editions but also includes some new
offerings.

In this new format, partly because of the larger
print, there are fewer words on any one page. There
is also more space around the words, giving more
room in which to make the prayer your own, as well
as more 'breathing space', perhaps even 'Spirit
space'. A friend who has been using a draft of this
revision found that the emptiness pointed to the reality of prayer being wider and deeper than the
words themselves. Also you are less anxious about
saying all the words without pausing, or about keeping track of where you have reached. You can look
up for a few seconds, or close your eyes, and easily
find your place again. Because you do not have to
search a page full of words (like this one!), you find
yourself less 'bound' to keep your eyes 'fixed' on the
text the whole time.

None of these prayers is meant to be set in stone.
If you make alterations in the margin you are making your own contribution to the living prayer of the

People of God, not desecrating an ancient monument. You may want to do this if you find yourself disagreeing with what is here. For example, one of the new prayers is 'Christ crucified' on p. 115. Lines 5–8 of that prayer draw on J. D. Crossan's research on what actually happened to the corpse of Jesus after his crucifixion. He concludes that it was highly unlikely that Jesus was buried in a tomb, let alone a rich man's tomb. If such a suggestion gives offence or seems nonsense, cross out the lines and maybe write your own. Even a gift book is not meant to be untouchable or unalterable.

So, too, with the image of the Unicorn in Sunday's Thanksgiving. Why unicorns? It has been the question I have most frequently been asked! Well, you never know when you are going to meet them. They are like angels – you may find yourself entertaining them unawares. Like angels too, they may bear messages from God. No one knows where they come from, nor how they reproduce. Perhaps they are beyond gender. They are vibrant, alive, and powerful creatures, yet also strangely pure and innocent. It has been said that only the 'virgin' can so attract unicorns that they come close enough for their wildness to be tamed. Some are depicted with spiralling horns – symbol of the integration of all that is apparently contradictory. And for medieval Europe the unicorn was a symbol for Christ, for the Gospel of Truth, and for Freedom.

PS to 'Puzzled of High Wycombe': Please do not take any of this too solemnly. Play with the unicorn. We don't have to *understand* everything. Why should we expect even God to make sense?

If that doesn't convince you, well, you can always use one of the images from the Thanksgiving on other days of the week: Evening Star (from Aotearoa / New Zealand), Snow Leopard (a shy, elusive creature, well camouflaged, much as God often seems to be), Albatross (think of the steady beat of powerful wings), Pilgrim Staff, Desert Bread, and Counsellor (the Holy Spirit in St John's Gospel). Where the images are not strictly scriptural, I trust they are consonant with the Scriptures.

The night might be dark, but it is also a time for wonder. And the fact that *A New Zealand Prayer Book* should have incorporated much of *Prayer at Night* (but not the unicorn!) brings vividly alive the marvel that every twenty-four hours are being prayed through as light and darkness move round our planet.

JIM COTTER

Sheffield, March 1997

SOURCES AND ACKNOWLEDGEMENTS

Some of the material is more or less the same for each day of the week. The first section of the *Invocation* is traditional, adapted by the Compiler. The second section varies and is a quotation from the Bible (Sunday: 1 Peter 5.8; Monday: Isaiah 40.31; Tuesday: John 4.24; Wednesday: 1 Corinthians 16.13–14; Thursday: Ephesians 6.18; Friday: Matthew 26.40–41; Saturday: Psalm 127.2. The third section is Psalm 121.2.

The *Thanksgiving* is almost the same each day of the week and is by the Compiler. The prayers of *Recognition* are mostly by the Compiler but draw largely on biblical sources. I know that the first prayers for Tuesday, Friday, and Saturday come from other people, but I have lost track of them: I apologize if I have infringed copyright. That for Wednesday could be given the title 'The Five New Testament Commandments'. The second of the prayers for Saturday is a re-working of the Collect for Purity at the beginning of the service of Holy Communion in the Book of Common Prayer.

The PSALMS are as follows:

Sunday: Psalm 103.1–18; a 'New Testament' Psalm by the Compiler.

Monday: Psalms 134; 4; 23.

Tuesday: Psalms 121; 16.7–11; 31.1–5.

Wednesday: Psalm 139.1–18.

Thursday: Psalms 46; 91.1–5,11,14–16.

Friday: Psalms 130; 126.

Saturday: Psalms 42; 43.

The READINGS are as follows:

Those for *Sunday* and *Monday* are paraphrases of the eight Beatitudes from Matthew 6. Those for the rest of the week are direct or slightly paraphrased quotations from the Bible:

Tuesday: Galatians 5.22–23; Luke 6.27–28, 35–38; Matthew 6.31–34; John 4.34.

Wednesday: 1 John 4.18–20; Jeremiah 14.9; 2 Corinthians 4.6–11; Ephesians 3.16–19.

Thursday: John 4.14; 2 Timothy 1.7; John 15.4 & 14.27; 1 Thessalonians 5.24.

Friday: John 15.12–13; Romans 8.14–17; Romans 8.19–23; Romans 8.38–39.

Saturday: 1 Timothy 6.6–8,10,11; Proverbs 31.8–9; 2 Corinthians 4.16-18; Isaiah 61.1-2.

The HYMNS are as follows:

Sunday: The ancient hymn, 'Phos Hilarion', a hymn written before the fourth century, this version by the Compiler.

Monday: Thomas Ken's hymn, adapted by the Compiler.

Tuesday: A hymn by Brian Wren, from his collection, *Bring Many Names*, printed here by permission of Stainer and Bell Ltd, © 1989 for the World except USA, Canada, Australia and New Zealand.

Wednesday: An old Latin hymn, adapted from the translation of J. M. Neale.

Thursday: Slightly adapted from Mrs C. F. Alexander's version of St Patrick's Breastplate.

Friday: By Charles Wesley.

Saturday: By the Compiler; it can be sung to the tune of *The Ash Grove*.

The PRAYERS are as follows:

'Into your hands' is from the Psalms.

'Antiphon' and 'Nunc Dimittis': the antiphon is traditional and the Nunc Dimittis a paraphrase of Luke 2.29–32.

The 'Kyries' are traditional.

'I will lie down in peace': the first section is from the Psalms, the second and third by the Compiler.

There are three versions of the Lord's Prayer,

two by the Compiler and the one for Friday inspired by Louis Evely's book, *Our Father*.

More specifically,

Sunday: 'Praying with Mary' and 'For this house' are by the Compiler; the Blessing is traditional.

Monday: 'For the blessings of touch' is by the Compiler; 'For joy' comes from a source that I haven't been able to trace; the Blessing is by the Compiler, with acknowledgement to Henry Vaughan for the phrase 'dazzling darkness'.

Tuesday: 'For peace' is the prayer for world peace written by Satish Kumar; 'For refreshment' is from the traditional version of Compline, slightly adapted; the Blessing is, I think, by William Temple.

Wednesday: 'For our work' is slightly adapted from a prayer by the great China scholar Joseph Needham; 'A greeting to our ancestors' is by the Compiler; the Blessing is from 2 Corinthians 13.14.

Thursday: 'For inner peace' is from the Book of Common Prayer; 'For the unity of humankind' is from a prayer written for an inter-faith gathering; the Blessing is by the Compiler.

Friday: 'Christ crucified' is by the Compiler; 'Lighten our darkness' is from the Book of Common Prayer, slightly adapted; the Blessing is by the Compiler.

Saturday: Both 'Loving God' and 'Abiding and increasing' are prayers adapted from two in the Book of Common Prayer; the Blessing is by the Compiler.

READINGS AND ANTIPHONS FOR SPECIAL DAYS
AND SEASONS:

Advent: Reading: Isaiah 40.3–5; Antiphon: Traditional.

Christmas: Reading: John 1.14, paraphrased; Antiphon: John 1.14.

Epiphany: Reading: Luke 2.30–32; Antiphon: Psalm 86.9.

Lent: Reading: Isaiah 58.6–8; Antiphon: John 17.19.

Passiontide: Reading: Isaiah 53.5; Antiphon: Philippians 2.7.

Easter: Reading: 1 Corinthians 15.20–22; Antiphon: Easter greeting.

Ascension: Reading: Based on Colossians 2.15; Antiphon: Based on Hebrews 12.2.

Pentecost: Reading: Romans 5.5; 2 Timothy 1.7; Antiphon: John 16.13.

Trinity: Reading: Revelation 4.8; 7.12; Antiphon: Compiler, owing the line 'Lover, Beloved, Mutual Friend' to Brian Wren's hymn acknowledged above.

Saints' Days: Reading: Revelation 1.17–18; 2.7, 10, 17; Antiphon: Based on Revelation 5.

The Departed: Reading: Alternative Service Book; Antiphon: Russian Kontakion.

ADDITIONAL PRAYERS

'God bless …': Compiler, the first section based on a prayer I came across in San Francisco.

'God be …': An extended, full-body, version of the traditional prayer, 'God be in my head'.

'To the troubling unknown': Compiler; the sections, 'The fauna of the night' and 'At the breaking of dawn' owe much to W. H. Auden's poem honouring Sigmund Freud; the section 'Encounter them' is based on Jacob's struggle with the stranger in Genesis 32.22–32; the section 'You are troubled by your dark angels' to the end is based on R. M. Rilke's words in his *Letters to a Young Poet* (Norton, New York, revised edition 1954).

'In the life of the city at night': Compiler, inspired by the view of the city of Sheffield from the chapel at the top of his house.

'A prayer of surrender' is based on one by Charles de Foucauld.

The three covenant prayers are by the Compiler. The prayer for 'friends, here and beyond' is based on one by John V. Taylor, whose inspiration for this and much else is gratefully acknowledged.

FOREWORD

Because of the changes of format in this edition, a few al-
terations have been made to the original Foreword that Jane
of the Sisters of the Love of God, an Anglican contempla-
tive community in Oxford, wrote when she was Mother of
the community. She died on St Patrick's Day in 1995 and is
much missed. Having, with her sisters, prayed much during
the hours of darkness (their Night Office is at 2 a.m.), she
can now perhaps be approached as the patron saint of all
those who pray as night approaches.

The Office of Compline is sometimes referred to as
'the goodnight prayer of the Church', with the im-
plication that it is a sort of liturgical lullaby round-
ing off the day and designed to ensure a quiet night.
This can be justified, as in the paraphrase of the
psalm in these pages: 'I will lie down in peace and
take my rest, for it is in God alone that I dwell unafraid.'

But praying at night involves considerably more
than a peaceful passage through the hours of darkness. We 'let go' into sleep just as, one day, we shall
have to 'let go' into death; and it is good to get
accustomed to something of what that surrender

involves. One of the prayers for Friday puts it acutely: '… give us courage to face what must decay, the disintegration of our mortal flesh, and give us faith to shed our false and deadly selves, to let them be as smoke vanishing in the evening breeze …'

The night hours are concerned with conflict as well as with quietness, and so preparation for them includes claiming the armour of God for spiritual struggle and filling our minds with a range of strong biblical imagery in order to make a positive affirmation that God is Love. We also need to be ready to explore what this statement means in itself and what it demands from us – an exercise which will not necessarily lead to comfort or reassurance.

Prayer in the night is different from prayer in the day. Whether it is 'waiting for the dawn' in the early hours, or 'doing battle' with the 'powers of evil' in the middle of the night, it requires a naked exposure before God – the kind of nakedness that can be clothed in the daytime by those familiar distractions which make it more difficult to stay still and keep attentive to God. So a liturgical office which is a gateway into the night needs to take account of this fact. Here we are given a form of Compline which is sharp as well as consoling in its reality and relevance. Based on the traditional pattern, it stands on its own, but could equally well fit into the daily cycle of the parochial or monastic office. The whole has undoubtedly emerged from the prayed experience of the Compiler, and so evokes a similar response in the user.

For example, the confessions (or 'recognitions'), different for each day of the week, taken together do not let us get away with the meaningless mutter that can, in a familiar formula, all too easily pass for penitence. Because on Friday and Saturday we spell out our nastiness and face its effect on other people, and we see just how our personal indifference and carelessness react negatively within the whole of creation, the more traditional phraseology of previous evenings comes alive, and the words have their intended impact. The choice of psalms, and the subtlety of the paraphrasing, both encourage and challenge us. There is a lot here about light piercing darkness, about mercy and forgiveness, about trust in God; above all, there is praise, worship, awe, in face of the 'Creator of the ever-changing hills'. God is our refuge and strength, and gives us gifts even while we sleep, but also the inescapable, all-knowing fashioner of 'cell and tissue, blood and bone' who searches us out and holds us, as in the palm of a hand.

Prayer at Night is authentic because in it the wisdom of the centuries, in scripture and above all in the psalms, is filled out with contemporary

Christian experience of God as 'Life-giver, Pain-bearer, Love-maker' – a phrase that makes us think what we mean when we use the more familiar Trinitarian formula – and the awareness that each of us who tries to pray is part of the human whole, subject to all manner of powers of darkness, including of course the ever-present threat of nuclear extinction.

So we are taken over the threshold from daytime, not in a holy huddle of 'me, myself, and God', but, whether prayed alone or in company, as representatives of humanity, acknowledging creaturehood before God – but also humbly grateful for our partnership with God in that loving work of redemption which 'pours our lifeblood in love for us', and indeed asks the same of us.

Jane, SLG

Oxford, 1983

HOW TO USE THIS BOOK

Some practical suggestions

Think 'simplicity' and think 'silence'. The prayers are neither complicated nor long. The lines are short, and the words on each page are surrounded by empty space so that they can breathe. Do not hurry. Pause often. Turn a page quickly only when in the middle of a psalm or prayer. (The pages are laid out deliberately so that you do not have to do this often.) Choose an uncluttered place in which to pray. Keep to one posture to encourage stillness. Let your backbone be straight, even if horizontal!

The book has four sections. The first provides all that you need for each night of the week, though you may sometimes wish to use the other three sections.

Turn to the day of the week. The sequence of the prayer is this:

· Invocation (opening yourself to God)
· Thanksgiving (glad about …)
· Recognition (sorry about …)
· Psalm(s) (praising and praying with

our ancestors)
- Reading (from the Bible; there are four to choose from: one is enough)
- Hymn (ancient and modern)
- Prayers (various)

When you have finished you might want to place one of the ribbons down the page so that you can easily find the beginning of the prayer for the following evening.

The second section provides material for special seasons and occasions, as variants for the everyday readings and antiphons to the Nunc Dimittis: Advent, Christmas, Epiphany, Lent, Passiontide, Easter, Ascension, Pentecost, Trinity, Saints' Days, The Departed. Put another ribbon down the appropriate page so that you can turn to it easily.

The third section is for particular prayers, for people and concerns close to your own heart: there are two blank pages for each day of the week for you to use as you wish. Turn to them when you reach the heading *PARTICULAR PRAYERS*. Again, a ribbon marking the place may be helpful.

The fourth section is for occasional use. Here are prayers of blessing, one looking outwards to city and world, one focusing on your own body. There is a meditative prayer concerned with all that rises to trouble and disturb us, often especially during the night. There is a litany so that you can bring to heart and mind those in the city who are awake while others sleep. And there are prayers of surrender and of covenant.

Lastly, the typography is designed to provide guidance:

· *ITALIC CAPITALS* indicate a new subdivision.
· ORDINARY CAPITALS indicate the beginning of a new prayer, psalm, or reading.
· **Bold letters** indicate 'everybody joins in'.
· Ordinary letters indicate the leader's part.
  (If you are praying on your own, simply ignore the difference between these last two.)
· Three dots, like this: … , suggest taking time to pause.
· Square brackets, like this: [ ], indicate the kind of prayer appropriate, but you have to supply your own words.

If you fall silent at any point, and you remain silent for the rest of the time you have put aside for the prayer, do not feel guilty about ending and not getting through all the words. Quality matters more than quantity. And, come to think of it, the chores you may still have to do before going to bed, like putting the cat or the milk bottles out, are also to be made part of our prayer at night's approaching.

SUNDAY

INVOCATION

THE angels of God guard us
through the night,
**and quieten
the powers of darkness.**

The Spirit of God
be our guide
to lead us to peace
and to glory.

PEOPLE of God, be sober, be watchful; your adversary the devil as a roaring lion prowls about, seeking someone to devour; whom withstand, steadfast in the faith.

OUR help is in the name
of the eternal God,
**who is making
the heavens and the earth.**

THANKSGIVING

DEAR God, thank you
for all that is good,
for our creation
and our humanity,
for the stewardship
you have given us
of this planet earth,
for the gifts of life
and of one another,

[for the people and events
of this day]

[for friends and family]

for your Love,
unbounded and eternal …

O Thou,
Most Holy and Beloved,
my Companion,
my Unicorn,
my Guide upon the Way.

RECOGNITION

WE have injured your love:
Binder of wounds, heal us.

We stumble in the darkness:
Light of the world, guide us.

We forget that we are your home:
Spirit of God, dwell in us ...

GOD of Joy,
we rejoice in you.

You run to meet us
like a welcoming friend,
you laugh with us
in the merriment of heaven,
you feast with us
at the great banquet,
Clown of clowns,
Fool of fools,
the only Entertainer of Jesters.

**God of Joy,
we rejoice in you.**

PSALMS

ETERNAL Spirit,
flow through our being
and open our lips,
**that our mouths
may proclaim your praise.**

Let us worship
the God of Love:
Alleluia. Alleluia.

FROM the deep places of my soul
I praise you, O God:
I lift up my heart
and glorify your holy name.
**From the deep places of my soul
I praise you, O God:
how can I forget
all your goodness towards me?**
You forgive all my sin,
you heal all my weakness,
**you rescue me
from the brink of disaster,
you crown me
with mercy and compassion.**

You satisfy my being
with good things,
so that my youth
is renewed like an eagle's.
**You fulfil
all that you promise,
justice
for all the oppressed.**
You made known
your ways to Moses,
and all the people
saw your deeds.
**You are full
of forgiveness and grace,
endlessly patient,
faithful in love.**
You do not haunt us
with our sins,
nor nurse grievances
against us.
**You do not repay
evil with evil,
for you are greater
than our sins.**
As vast as the heavens are
in comparison with the earth,

so great is your love
to those who trust you.
As far as the east is
from the west,
so far do you fling
our sins from us.
Just as parents
are merciful to their children,
so are you merciful
and kind towards us.
For you know
how fragile we are,
that we are made
of the dust of the earth.
Our days are
like the grass,
they bloom like
the flowers of the field.
The wind blows over them
and they are gone,
and no one can tell
where they stood.
Only your merciful goodness
endures:
age after age
you act justly

**towards all who hold on
to your covenant,
who take your words to heart
and fulfil them.**

FOR you have triumphed
over the power of death,
and draw us to your presence
with songs of joy.
**We hear the echo of your angels
praising you,
and the whole communion
of your saints,**
those who have walked
in your narrow ways,
and heard the voice
of your yearning,
**whose food
is to do your will
and in whom
you take great delight.**
From the widest bounds
of the universe
to the depths
of my very being,

**the whispers and cries of joy
vibrate to a shining glory,
O God,
our beginning and our end.**

READING

Poverty

WRETCHED are those
who crave more and more possessions:
they will be crushed by the weight
and burden of them.

Blessed are those
who are ready to do without,
to be empty, to be nothing,
to be humble and open to receive,
knowing their need of God:
they have found the secret of living,
and are rich indeed …

Grief

WRETCHED are those
who wallow in self-pity:
they will sink into bitterness and despair.

Blessed are those
who accept their experience of sorrow:
they will grow in courage and compassion.

Struggle

WRETCHED are those
who have ceased to care
and be disturbed,
and are now too much at ease:
they will be bored,
and will disintegrate into dust.

Blessed are those
who hunger and thirst and strive
for what is just and good:
they will be made whole,
and will be well content …

Insecurity

WRETCHED are those
who, in their insecurity,
look anxiously for appreciation
from others:
they claim everything for themselves,
and yet possess nothing,
wandering unhappily
and belonging nowhere.

Blessed are those
who have accepted their insecurity,
and are content to go unrecognized
and unrewarded,
claiming nothing for themselves:
the freedom of the earth is theirs;
never exiled,
they are everywhere at home ...

HYMN

HAIL, gladdening Light,
of God's pure glory poured,
Who is the great Creator,
heavenly, blest,
Holiest of holies,
Jesus Christ who reigns.

Now we are come
to the sun's hour of rest,
The lights of evening
round us shine,
We hymn the God of Love,
Eternal Spirit divine.

You are worthy, O God,
at all times to be sung,
With clear and truthful voice,
Light of Light,
Giver of life, alone!
Therefore in all the world
your glories, Christ, we own.

INTO YOUR HANDS

INTO your hands
I commend the whole of my being,
**for you have redeemed me,
body and soul,
O God of truth and love.**

Keep me, dear God,
as the apple of an eye,
**hide me under the shadow
of your wings.**

ANTIPHON TO THE NUNC DIMITTIS

PRESERVE us,
dear God,
while waking,
and guard us
while sleeping,
that awake
we may watch
with Christ,
and asleep
we may rest
in your peace.

NUNC DIMITTIS

PRAISE be to God,
I have lived to see this day.
God's promise is fulfilled,
and my duty done.

At last you have given me peace,
for I have seen with my own eyes
the salvation you have prepared
for all nations,
a light to the world
in its darkness,
and the glory
of your people Israel.

Glory be to God,
sustaining, redeeming, sanctifying,
as in the beginning,
so now, and for ever. Amen.

KYRIES

Kyrie eleison
Christe eleison
Kyrie eleison

PRAYING IN CHRIST

ETERNAL Spirit,
Life-Giver,
Pain-Bearer,
Love-Maker,
Source of all that is
and that shall be,
Father and Mother
of us all,
Loving God,
in whom is heaven:

The Hallowing of your Name
echo through the universe.
The Way of your Justice
be followed
by the peoples of the world.
Your Heavenly Will be done
by all created beings.
Your Commonwealth
of Peace and Freedom
sustain our hope
and come on earth.

With the bread
we need for today
　　feed us.
In the hurts
we absorb from one another
　　forgive us.
In times of temptation
and test,
　　strengthen us.
From trials too sharp
to endure,
　　spare us.
From the grip
of all that is evil,
　　free us.

For you reign in the glory
of the power that is love,
now and for ever. Amen.

I WILL LIE DOWN IN PEACE

I WILL lie down in peace
and take my rest,
**for it is in God alone
that I dwell unafraid.**

Let us bless the Life-Giver,
the Pain-Bearer, the Love-Maker;
**let us praise and exalt God
above all for ever.**

May God's name be praised
beyond the furthest star,
**glorified and exalted
above all for ever.**

[PARTICULAR PRAYERS]

PRAYING WITH MARY

REJOICING with you,
grieving with you,

Mary, graced by God –
Love's Mystery did come to you –
of our race we deem you
most the blessed,

save but the Blessed One,
the Child
who came to birth in you.

Woman holy,

trembling at the Presence
of the Angel,

willing the rare
and marvellous exchange,

in the darkness
holding the Unseen,

bearing forth
the Word made flesh
for earth's redeeming,

hold to your heart our world,
and pray for humankind,

that we with you
be bearers of the Christ,

through this
and all our days,
and at the last.

FOR THIS HOUSE

BE present, Living Christ,
within us,
your dwelling place and home,
that this house
may be one
where our darkness
is penetrated by your light,
where our troubles
are calmed by your peace,
where our evil
is redeemed by your love,
where our pain
is transformed in your suffering,
and where our dying
is glorified in your risen life.

BLESSING

GOD of love and mercy,
grant us, with all your people,
rest and peace.

The divine Spirit dwells in us:
Thanks be to God.

MONDAY

INVOCATION

THE angels of God guard us
through the night,
**and quieten
the powers of darkness.**

The Spirit of God
be our guide
**to lead us to peace
and to glory.**

THEY that wait for the Spirit shall renew their
strength: they shall mount up with wings as eagles,
they shall run and not be weary, they shall walk and
not faint.

OUR help is in the name
of the eternal God,
**who is making
the heavens and the earth.**

THANKSGIVING

DEAR God, thank you
for all that is good,
for our creation
and our humanity,
for the stewardship
you have given us
of this planet earth,
for the gifts of life
and of one another,

[for the people and events
of this day]

[for all with whom we have to do in our
communities]

for your Love,
unbounded and eternal …

O Thou,
Most Holy and Beloved,
my Companion,
my Evening Star,
my Guide upon the Way.

RECOGNITION

WE grieve and confess

**that we harm
and have been harmed,**

**to the third
and fourth generations,**

**that we are so afraid of pain
that we shield ourselves
from being vulnerable to others,**

**and refuse to be open
and trusting as a child …**

GOD of Wholeness,
we rest in you.

You listen with us
to the sound
of running water,

you sit with us
under the shade
of the trees of our healing,

you walk once more with us
in the garden
in the cool of the day,

the oil of your anointing
penetrates the cells
of our being,

the warmth of your hands
touches us kindly,
steadies us
and gives us courage.

**God of Wholeness,
we rest in you.**

PSALMS

ETERNAL Spirit,
flow through our being
and open our lips,
**that our mouths
may proclaim your praise.**

Let us worship
the God of Love:
Alleluia. Alleluia.

WE your servants
bless you, dear God,
as we stand by night
in your house.
**We lift up our hands
towards the holy place,
and give you
thanks and praise.**
Bless us from all places
where you dwell,
**O God, Creator
of the heavens and the earth.**

ANSWER me
when I call, O God,
for you are the God
of Justice.
**You set me free
when I was hard-pressed:
be gracious to me now
and hear my prayer.**
Men and women,
how long will you turn my glory
to my shame?
How long will you love
what is worthless,
and run after lies?
**Know that God has shown me
such wonderful kindness:
when I call out in prayer,
God hears me.**
Tremble, admit defeat,
and sin no more.
Look deep into your heart
before you sleep,
and be still.
**Bring your gifts,
just as you are,
and put your trust in God.**

Many are asking,
Who can make us content?
The light of your countenance
has gone from us, O God.
Yet you have given my heart
more gladness
than those whose corn and wine
and oil increase.
I will lie down in peace
and sleep comes at once,
for in you alone, O God,
do I dwell unafraid.

DEAR God,
you sustain me and feed me:
like a shepherd
you guide me.
You lead me
to an oasis of green,
to lie down
by restful waters.
You refresh my soul
for the journey,
and guide me
along trusted roads.

**Though I must enter
the darkness of death,
I will fear no evil.
For you are with me,
your rod and your staff
comfort me.**
You prepare a table
before my very eyes,
in the presence of those
who trouble me.
**You anoint my head
with oil,
and you fill my cup
to the brim.**
Your lovingkindness and mercy
will meet me
every day of my life,
**and I will dwell
in the house of my God
for ever.**

READING

Love

WRETCHED are those
who show no compassion
and are insensitive
to the needs of others:
they will always complain
of being misunderstood,
and they will never be loved.

Blessed are those
who accept and forgive
those who hurt them:
they will find understanding
and love.

Truth

WRETCHED are those
who live in illusion
and fantasy:
they will be utterly lost.

Blessed are those
who are honest with themselves,
who are being refined
and chastened,
and seek to live the truth:
they will know themselves
and they will know God.

Peace

WRETCHED are those
who are at war with themselves,
who spread evil and division
and hatred,
seeking to dominate others:
they breed their own downfall,
and they never know trust
and friendship.

Blessed are those
who create reconciliation
and goodwill
wherever they go,
returning good for evil:
they are indeed the friends of God.

Life

WRETCHED are those
whose lives are shallow
and full of fear,
who cannot respond in truth
when they are challenged:
they will freeze in death.

Blessed are those
who shed their pettiness,
and know the deep things of God
and of themselves,
and so persevere
at whatever the cost –
insult, slander, exile, death:
they will have life
and know it abundantly.

HYMN

GLORY to you, my God, this night,
For all the blessings of the light,
To you, from whom all good does come,
Our life, our health, our lasting home.

Teach me to live, that I may dread
The grave as little as my bed.
Teach me to die, that so I may
Rise glorious at the aweful day.

O may I now on you repose,
And may kind sleep my eyelids close,
Sleep that may me more vigorous make
To serve my God when I awake.

If I lie restless on my bed,
Your word of healing peace be said.
If powerful dreams rise in the night,
Transform their darkness into light.

All praise to God, sustaining us,
Redeeming and transfiguring us,
Thanksgiving in eternity,
All praise, beloved Trinity.

INTO YOUR HANDS

INTO your hands
I commend the whole of my being,
**for you have redeemed me,
body and soul,
O God of truth and love.**

Keep me, dear God,
as the apple of an eye,
**hide me under the shadow
of your wings.**

ANTIPHON TO THE NUNC DIMITTIS

PRESERVE us,
dear God,
while waking,
and guard us
while sleeping,
that awake
we may watch
with Christ,
and asleep
we may rest
in your peace.

NUNC DIMITTIS

PRAISE be to God,
I have lived to see this day.
God's promise is fulfilled,
and my duty done.

At last you have given me peace,
for I have seen with my own eyes
the salvation you have prepared
for all nations,
a light to the world
in its darkness,
and the glory
of your people Israel.

Glory be to God,
sustaining, redeeming, sanctifying,
as in the beginning,
so now, and for ever. Amen.

KYRIES

KYRIE eleison
Christe eleison
Kyrie eleison

PRAYING IN CHRIST

ABBA, Amma, Beloved ...
your name be hallowed ...
your reign spread among us ...
your will be done well ...
at all times, in all places ...
on earth, as in heaven ...

Give us the bread ...
we need for today ...
Forgive us our trespass ...
as we forgive those ...
who trespass against us ...
Let us not fail ...
in time of our testing ...
Spare us from trials ...
too sharp to endure ...
Free us from the grip ...
of all evil powers ...

For yours is the reign ...
the power and the glory ...
the victory of love ...
for time and eternity ...
world without end ...
So be it. Amen ...

I WILL LIE DOWN IN PEACE

I WILL lie down in peace
and take my rest,
**for it is in God alone
that I dwell unafraid.**

Let us bless the Life-Giver,
the Pain-Bearer, the Love-Maker;
**let us praise and exalt God
above all for ever.**

May God's name be praised
beyond the furthest star,
**glorified and exalted
above all for ever.**

[PARTICULAR PRAYERS]

FOR THE BLESSINGS OF TOUCH

GIVER of life,
Bearer of pain,
Maker of love,
affirming in your incarnation
the goodness of the flesh,
may the yearnings of our bodies
be fulfilled in sacraments of love,
and our earthly embracings
a foretaste of the pleasure
that shall be,
in the glory
of the resurrection body
of Jesus Christ.

FOR JOY

DEAR God,
the Source
of the whole world's gladness,
and the Bearer
of its pain,
may your unconquerable joy
rest at the heart
of all our trouble and distress.

BLESSING

FRIEND and Lover,
bless us and keep us;
Light of the world,
shine on our faces;
Transfigured Yeshua,
lift us to glory.
May the darkness of night
deepen and dazzle.

The divine Spirit
dwells in us:
Thanks be to God.

TUESDAY

INVOCATION

THE angels of God guard us
through the night,
**and quieten
the powers of darkness.**

The Spirit of God
be our guide
**to lead us to peace
and to glory.**

GOD is spirit and those who worship God must
worship in spirit and in truth.

OUR help is in the name
of the eternal God,
**who is making
the heavens and the earth.**

THANKSGIVING

DEAR God, thank you
for all that is good,
for our creation
and our humanity,
for the stewardship
you have given us
of this planet earth,
for the gifts of life
and of one another,

[for the people and events
of this day]

[for this neighbourhood/
village/town/city]

for your Love,
unbounded and eternal ...

O Thou,
Most Holy and Beloved,
my Companion,
my Snow Leopard,
my Guide upon the Way.

RECOGNITION

MERCIFUL God,
we have not loved you
with our whole heart,
nor our neighbours
as ourselves.

Forgive what we have been,
accept us as we are,
and guide what we shall be …

GOD of Mercy,
we thank you.

You forgive our past sin,
you bless us abundantly,
you give us new strength,
you fill us with gratitude,
you sow in us seeds of new life,
you shape us for glory.

God of Mercy,
we thank you.

PSALM

ETERNAL Spirit,
flow through our being
and open our lips,
**that our mouths
may proclaim your praise.**

Let us worship
the God of Love:
Alleluia. Alleluia.

I WILL lift up my eyes
to the mountains,
but where
shall I find help?
**From you alone, O God,
does my help come,
Creator
of the ever-changing hills.**
You will not let me stumble
on the rough pathways,
you care for me and
watch over me without ceasing.

I am sure
that the Guardian of Israel
neither slumbers
nor sleeps.
The God of all peoples
keeps watch,
like a shadow
spread over me.
So the sun
will not strike me
by day,
nor the moon by night.
You will defend me
in the presence of evil,
you will guard my life.
You will defend
my going out
and my coming in,
this night and always.

DEAR God, I give you thanks
for the wisdom of your counsel,
even at night
you have instructed my heart.

I have set your face
always before me,
you are at my right hand
and I shall not fall.
Therefore my heart is glad
and my spirit rejoices,
my flesh also
shall rest secure.
For you will not give me over
to the power of death,
nor let your faithful one
see the Pit.
In your presence
is the fulness of joy,
and from your right hand
flow delights for evermore.

DEAR God,
I have come to you
for shelter:
let me never
be put to shame.
Deliver me in the justice
of your ways:
incline your ear to me
and save me.

Be for me a rock of refuge,
a fortress to defend me,
for you are my rock
and my stronghold.
**Lead me and guide me
for your name's sake:
deliver me out of the net
that they have laid secretly for me
for you are my strength.**
Into your hands
I commit my spirit,
**for you will redeem me,
eternal God of Truth.**

READING

THE fruit of the Spirit
is love, joy, peace,
patience, kindness, goodness,
faithfulness, gentleness, self-discipline …

If we live by the Spirit,
let us also walk by the Spirit …

and bear one another's burdens,
and so fulfil the law of Christ …

LOVE your enemies …

Do good to those who hate you.
Bless those who curse you.
Pray for those who abuse you …

Do good and lend,
expecting nothing in return …

For God is kind
to the ungrateful and selfish …

Be merciful as your Father is merciful.
Judge not and you will not be judged.
Condemn not and you not be condemned.
Forgive and you will be forgiven.
Give, and it will be given to you …

For the measure you give
will be the measure you receive …

DO not ask anxiously,
What are we to eat?
What are we to drink?
What shall we wear? ...

The whole heathen world
runs after such things ...

Set your heart and mind
on God's Commonwealth first,
and all the rest will come to you as well ...

So do not be anxious about tomorrow.
Today has enough problems of its own.
Tomorrow can look after itself ...

MY food is to do the will
of the One who sent me,
to accomplish God's work ...

I have food to eat
of which you do not know ...

HYMN

HOW wonderful the Three-in-One,
Whose energies of dancing light
Are undivided, pure and good,
Communing love in shared delight.

Before the flow of dawn and dark,
Creation's Lover dreamed of earth,
And with a caring deep and wise,
All things conceived and brought to birth.

The Lover's own Belov'd, in time,
Between a cradle and a cross,
At home in flesh, gave love and life
To heal our brokenness and loss.

Their Equal Friend all life sustains
With greening power and loving care,
And calls us, born again by grace,
In Love's communing life to share.

How wonderful the Living God:
Divine Beloved, Empow'ring Friend,
Eternal Lover, Three-in-One,
Our hope's beginning, way, and end.

INTO YOUR HANDS

INTO your hands
I commend the whole of my being,
for you have redeemed me,
body and soul,
O God of truth and love.

Keep me, dear God,
as the apple of an eye,
hide me under the shadow
of your wings.

ANTIPHON TO THE NUNC DIMITTIS

PRESERVE us,
dear God,
while waking,
and guard us
while sleeping,
that awake
we may watch
with Christ,
and asleep
we may rest
in your peace.

NUNC DIMITTIS

PRAISE be to God,
I have lived to see this day.
God's promise is fulfilled,
and my duty done.

At last you have given me peace,
for I have seen with my own eyes
the salvation you have prepared
for all nations,
a light to the world
in its darkness,
and the glory
of your people Israel.

Glory be to God,
sustaining, redeeming, sanctifying,
as in the beginning,
so now, and for ever. Amen.

KYRIES

KYRIE eleison
Christe eleison
Kyrie eleison

PRAYING IN CHRIST

**ETERNAL Spirit,
Life-Giver,
Pain-Bearer,
Love-Maker,
Source of all that is
and that shall be,
Father and Mother
of us all,
Loving God,
in whom is heaven:**

**The Hallowing of your Name
echo through the universe.
The Way of your Justice
be followed
by the peoples of the world.
Your Heavenly Will be done
by all created beings.
Your Commonwealth
of Peace and Freedom
sustain our hope
and come on earth.**

With the bread
we need for today
    feed us.
In the hurts
we absorb from one another
    forgive us.
In times of temptation
and test,
    strengthen us.
From trials too sharp
to endure,
    spare us.
From the grip
of all that is evil,
    free us.

For you reign in the glory
of the power that is love,
now and for ever. Amen.

I WILL LIE DOWN IN PEACE

I WILL lie down in peace
and take my rest,
**for it is in God alone
that I dwell unafraid.**

Let us bless the Life-Giver,
the Pain-Bearer, the Love-Maker;
**let us praise and exalt God
above all for ever.**

May God's name be praised
beyond the furthest star,
**glorified and exalted
above all for ever.**

[PARTICULAR PRAYERS]

FOR PEACE

GOD of many names,
Lover of all peoples,
we pray for peace,
in our hearts,
in our homes,
in our nations,
in our world,
the peace of your will,
the peace of our need.

FOR REFRESHMENT

BE present, Spirit of God,
and renew us
through the silent hours
of this night,
so that we who are wearied
by the changes and chances
of this fleeting world,
may rest upon
your eternal changelessness;
in the Spirit of Jesus Christ,
our Guardian and our Guide.

BLESSING

TO God the Creator
who loved us first
and gave this world
to be our home:

To God the Redeemer
who loves us
and by dying and rising
pioneered the way of freedom:

To God the Sanctifier
who spreads the divine love
in our hearts:

be praise and glory
for time and for eternity.

The divine Spirit
dwells in us:
Thanks be to God.

WEDNESDAY

INVOCATION

THE angels of God guard us
through the night,
**and quieten
the powers of darkness.**

The Spirit of God
be our guide
**to lead us to peace
and to glory.**

BE alert; stand firm in the faith; be courageous and
strong. Let everything you do be done in love.

OUR help is in the name
of the eternal God
**who is making
the heavens and the earth.**

THANKSGIVING

DEAR God, thank you
for all that is good,
for our creation
and our humanity,
for the stewardship
you have given us
of this planet earth,
for the gifts of life
and of one another,

[for the people and events
of this day]

[for our ancestors, for the
land, for this country]

for your Love,
unbounded and eternal ...

O Thou,
Most Holy and Beloved,
my Companion,
my Albatross,
my Guide upon the Way.

RECOGNITION

HEAR the wisdom of Jesus:

Abide in my love.
Kyrie eleison.

Love your enemies.
Christe eleison.

Love your neighbour
as yourself.
Kyrie eleison.

Love one another
as I have loved you.
Christe eleison.

Above all,
love God
with the whole
of your being.
Kyrie eleison …

GOD of Forgiveness,
we contemplate you.

You pour out
your lifeblood
in love for us,

you pursue us
and disturb us
and accept us,

you take to your heart
our sin and pain,
the gift of a costly
and infinite endurance,

you overcome evil
with the goodness
of love.

**God of Forgiveness,
we contemplate you.**

PSALM

ETERNAL Spirit,
flow through our being
and open our lips,
**that our mouths
may proclaim your praise**.

Let us worship
the God of Love:
Alleluia. Alleluia.

LIGHT of Light,
you have searched me out
and found me.
**You know where I am
and where I go,
you see my thoughts
from afar.**
You discern my paths
and my resting places,
you are acquainted
with all my ways.

**Yes, and not a word
comes from my lips
but you, O God,
have heard it already.**
You are in front of me
and you are behind me,
you have laid your hand
on my shoulder.
**Such knowledge
is too wonderful for me,
so great
that I cannot fathom it.**
Where shall I go
from your Spirit?
Where shall I flee
from your Presence?
**If I climb to the heavens
you are there:
if I descend to the depths
of the ocean,
you are there also.**
If I spread my wings
towards the morning,
and fly to the uttermost shores
of the sea,

even there your hand
will lead me,
and your right hand
will hold me.
If I should cry to the darkness
to cover me,
and the night
to enclose me,
even the darkness is
no darkness to you,
and the night is
as clear as the day.
For you have created
every part of my being,
cell and tissue,
blood and bone.
You have woven me
in the womb of my mother;
I will praise you,
so wonderfully am I made.
You know me to the very core
of my being;
nothing in me was hidden
from your eyes

**when I was formed
in silence and secrecy,
in intricate splendour
in the depths of the earth.**
Even as they were forming,
you saw my limbs,
each part of my body
shaped by your finger.
**How deep are your thoughts
to me, O God,
how great
is the sum of them.**
Were I to count them
they are more in number
than the grains of sand
upon the sea-shore –
**and still I would know
nothing about you –
yet still would you hold me
in the palm of your hand.**

READING

THERE is no fear in love,
but perfect love casts out fear.
For fear has to do with punishment,
and those who are afraid
are not perfected in love.
We love because God first loved us.
If anyone says, I love God,
and hates a brother or sister,
that person is a liar;
for those who do not love their brothers
    and sisters
whom they have seen
cannot love God
whom they have not seen.

LIVING God,
you are in the midst of us,
and we are called
by your holy name;
leave us not,
O God of Love.

IT is the God who said,
Let light shine
out of darkness,
who has shone
in our hearts
to give the light
of the knowledge
of the glory of God
in the face of Jesus Christ.
But we have this treasure
in earthen vessels,
to show that the transcendent power
belongs to God and not to us.
We are afflicted in every way,
but not crushed;
perplexed,
but not driven to despair;
persecuted,
but not forsaken;
struck down,
but not destroyed;
always carrying in the body
the death of Jesus,
so that the life of Jesus
may also be manifested
in our bodies.

ACCORDING to the riches
of God's glory,
may we be strengthened
with might
through the Holy Spirit
in our inner being,
that being rooted
and grounded in love,
we may have power
to comprehend,
with all the saints,
what is the breadth
and length and height
and depth,
and to know
the love of God
which surpasses knowledge,
that we may be filled
with all the fulness of God.

HYMN

BEFORE the ending of the day,
Creator of the world we pray,
That you, with love and lasting light,
Would guard us through the hours of night.

From all ill dreams defend our eyes,
From nightly fears and fantasies,
Redeem through us our evil foe,
That we no lasting harm may know.

O Wisest Guide grant all we ask,
Fulfil in us your holy task,
Surround us with your love and care,
And lead us on, your life to share.

All praise to God, sustaining us,
Redeeming and transfiguring us,
Thanksgiving in eternity,
All praise, beloved Trinity.

INTO YOUR HANDS

INTO your hands
I commend the whole of my being,
**for you have redeemed me,
body and soul,
O God of truth and love**.

Keep me, dear God,
as the apple of an eye,
**hide me under the shadow
of your wings.**

ANTIPHON TO THE NUNC DIMITTIS

PRESERVE us,
dear God,
while waking,
and guard us
while sleeping,
that awake
we may watch
with Christ,
and asleep
we may rest
in your peace.

NUNC DIMITTIS

PRAISE be to God,
I have lived to see this day.
God's promise is fulfilled,
and my duty done.

At last you have given me peace,
for I have seen with my own eyes
the salvation you have prepared
for all nations,
a light to the world
in its darkness,
and the glory
of your people Israel.

Glory be to God,
sustaining, redeeming, sanctifying,
as in the beginning,
so now, and for ever. Amen.

KYRIES

KYRIE eleison
Christe eleison
Kyrie eleison

PRAYING IN CHRIST

ABBA, Amma, Beloved …
your name be hallowed …
your reign spread among us …
your will be done well …
at all times, in all places …
on earth, as in heaven …

Give us the bread …
we need for today …
Forgive us our trespass …
as we forgive those …
who trespass against us …
Let us not fail …
in time of our testing …
Spare us from trials …
too sharp to endure …
Free us from the grip …
of all evil powers …

For yours is the reign …
the power and the glory …
the victory of love …
for time and eternity …
world without end …
So be it. Amen …

I WILL LIE DOWN IN PEACE

I WILL lie down in peace
and take my rest,
**for it is in God alone
that I dwell unafraid.**

Let us bless the Life-Giver,
the Pain-Bearer, the Love-Maker;
**let us praise and exalt God
above all for ever.**

May God's name be praised
beyond the furthest star,
**glorified and exalted
above all for ever.**

[PARTICULAR PRAYERS]

FOR OUR WORK

O GOD,
whose glory shines
through the heavens,
and whose handiwork
the universe declares,
may all the peoples
and workers of the world
be emancipated from
the kingdom of mammon
and all labour
and craftsmanship
become a work of ministry
in your kingdom of grace;
through Jesus Christ our Lord.

A GREETING TO OUR ANCESTORS

THE God of peace
sanctify you completely,
even to the glory
of the great day:
faithful is the God who calls,
the God whose promises
will be fulfilled.

NN,
**God bless you richly,
grow in grace,
make love,
keep us in loving mind,
hold us close in the Presence,
guide us,
pray for us.**

BLESSING

THE grace of Jesus Christ,
the love of God,
and communion
in the Holy Spirit,
be with us
now and always.

The divine Spirit
dwells in us:
Thanks be to God.

THURSDAY

INVOCATION

THE angels of God guard us
through the night,
**and quieten
the powers of darkness.**

The Spirit of God
be our guide
**to lead us to peace
and to glory.**

PRAY in the power of the Spirit. Keep watch and
persevere, and remember all God's people.

OUR help is in the name
of the eternal God,
**who is making
the heavens and the earth.**

THANKSGIVING

DEAR God, thank you
for all that is good,
for our creation
and our humanity,
for the stewardship
you have given us
of this planet earth,
for the gifts of life
and of one another,

[for the people and events
of this day]

[for all the world's peoples
and faiths]

for your Love,
unbounded and eternal ...

O Thou,
Most Holy and Beloved,
my Companion,
my Pilgrim Staff,
my Guide upon the Way.

RECOGNITION

LOVING God,
close your eyes to our sins,
**we who have wounded
your love.**

Refine us with the flame
of your Spirit:
**cleanse us with springs
of living water.**

Save us with words
of forgiveness and peace:
**make us whole,
steadfast in spirit.**

Broken are our bones,
yet you can heal us,
**and we shall leap for joy
and dance again …**

GOD of Love,
we adore you

You transfigure
our disfigured faces,

you strive
with our resistant clay,

you bring
out of our chaos, harmony.

**God of Love,
we adore you.**

PSALMS

Eternal Spirit,
flow through our being
and open our lips,
**that our mouths
may proclaim your praise.**

Let us worship
the God of Love:
Alleluia. Alleluia.

GOD is our refuge
and strength,
a very present help
in time of trouble.
**Therefore we shall not
be afraid,
even though the earth
be moved,**
even though the mountains
should crumble
and fall into the sea,
even though the waters
should foam and rage,
assault the cliffs
and make them shudder.
**You are for us
the God of the powers,
a safe stronghold,
the God of all peoples.**

There is a river
whose streams make glad
the city of God.
Here is God's dwelling place
and it will stand firm.

**God's rescue dawns
like the morning light,
God's voice echoes
through every land.**
When powerful nations
panic and totter,
and the whole world
comes crashing down,
**You are for us
the God of the powers,
a safe stronghold,
the God of all peoples.**

Come and see,
stand in awe
at the powerful things
God will do on the earth,
**putting an end
to all war in the world,
breaking the bow,
shattering the spear
into splinters,
throwing our weapons
on the fire.**

Be still
and know that I am God:
exalted among the nations,
my name known at last
on the earth.
**You are for us
the God of the powers,
a safe stronghold,
the God of all peoples.**

THEY who dwell in the shelter
of the Most High,
who abide under the shadow
of the Almighty,
say to our God,
**You are my refuge
and stronghold,
my God in whom
I put my trust.**
You set me free
from the snare
of the hunter,
and from evil's
destroying curse.

**You cover me
with your wings,
and I shall be safe
under your feathers.
Your faithfulness shall be
my shield and defence.**
In the dead of night
I have no terror to fear,
neither dread in the daytime
the plunge of the dagger,
**nor fear the plague
that stalks in the darkness,
nor the fever that strikes
in the heat of the day.**
For you, O God,
will command your angels
to keep me
in your narrow ways:
**they will bear me up
in their hands,
lest I dash my foot
against a stone.**
Because I am bound to you
in love,
therefore
I will deliver you.

**I will lift you
out of danger
because you hold on
to my name.**
In your anguish and need
I am with you,
I will set you free
and clothe you with glory.
**You will live
to be full of years,
and you will know
the abundance of my salvation**.

READING

THOSE who drink the water
that I shall give them
shall never thirst:
it will become in them
a bubbling spring,
welling up to eternal life.

GOD has not given us
a spirit of fear,
but of power
and of love
and of a sound mind.

ABIDE in me
and I in you:
as the branch
cannot bear fruit
of itself,
unless it abides
in the vine,
neither can you
unless you abide
in me ...

Peace I leave with you,
my peace I give to you.
Let not your hearts
be troubled,
neither let them
be afraid.

THE God who calls you is faithful.
The same God will enable you,
fulfilling the promise of old.

HYMN

Be thou my vision,
O Christ of my heart,
Be all else but naught to me,
Save that thou art,
Be thou my best thought
In the day and the night,
Both waking and sleeping,
Thy presence my light.

Riches I heed not,
Nor vain empty praise,
Be thou my inheritance
Now and always.
Be thou and thou only
The first in my heart,
O Sovereign of heaven,
My treasure thou art.

INTO YOUR HANDS

INTO your hands
I commend the whole of my being,
For you have redeemed me,
body and soul,
O God of truth and love.

Keep me, dear God,
as the apple of an eye,
hide me under the shadow
of your wings.

ANTIPHON TO THE NUNC DIMITTIS

PRESERVE us,
dear God,
while waking,
and guard us
while sleeping,
that awake
we may watch
with Christ,
and asleep
we may rest
in your peace.

NUNC DIMITTIS

PRAISE be to God,
I have lived to see this day.
God's promise is fulfilled,
and my duty done.

At last you have given me peace,
for I have seen with my own eyes
the salvation you have prepared
for all nations,
a light to the world
in its darkness,
and the glory
of your people Israel.

Glory be to God,
sustaining, redeeming, sanctifying,
as in the beginning,
so now, and for ever. Amen.

KYRIES

KYRIE eleison
Christe eleison
Kyrie eleison

PRAYING IN CHRIST

ETERNAL Spirit,
Life-Giver,
Pain-Bearer,
Love-Maker,
Source of all that is
and that shall be,
Father and Mother
of us all,
Loving God,
in whom is heaven:

The Hallowing of your Name
echo through the universe.
The Way of your Justice
be followed
by the peoples of the world.
Your Heavenly Will be done
by all created beings.
Your Commonwealth
of Peace and Freedom
sustain our hope
and come on earth.

With the bread
we need for today
   feed us.
In the hurts
we absorb from one another
   forgive us.
In times of temptation
and test,
   strengthen us.
From trials too sharp
to endure,
   spare us.
From the grip
of all that is evil,
   free us.

For you reign in the glory
of the power that is love,
now and for ever. Amen.

I WILL LIE DOWN IN PEACE

I WILL lie down in peace
and take my rest,
**for it is in God alone
that I dwell unafraid.**

Let us bless the Life-Giver,
the Pain-Bearer, the Love-Maker;
**let us praise and exalt God
above all for ever.**

May God's name be praised
beyond the furthest star,
**glorified and exalted
above all for ever**.

[PARTICULAR PRAYERS]

FOR INNER PEACE

O GOD,
from whom
all holy desires,
all good counsels,
and all just works
do proceed,
give unto thy servants
that peace
which the world
cannot give,
that our hearts
may be set
to obey
thy commandments,
and also that by thee,
we being defended
from the fear
of our enemies,
may pass our time
in rest and quietness;
through the merits
of Jesus Christ
our Saviour.

FOR THE UNITY OF HUMANKIND

WE adore thee,
who art One
and who art Love;
and it is in unity and love
that we would live together,
doing thy will.

BLESSING

THE blessing of God,
Giver of Life,
Bearer of Pain,
Maker of Love,
be with us
now and always.

The divine Spirit
dwells in us:
Thanks be to God.

FRIDAY

INVOCATION

THE angels of God guard us
through the night,
and quieten
the powers of darkness.

The Spirit of God
be our guide
to lead us to peace
and to glory.

JESUS said to his disciples, Were you not able to
stay awake for one hour? Keep watch all of you,
and pray that you will not fail in time of testing.

OUR help is in the name
of the eternal God,
who is making
the heavens and the earth.

THANKSGIVING

DEAR God, thank you
for all that is good,
for our creation
and our humanity,
for the stewardship
you have given us
of this planet earth,
for the gifts of life
and of one another,

[for the people and events
of this day]

[for all that you have given us
through Jesus of Nazareth]

for your Love,
unbounded and eternal ...

O Thou,
Most Holy and Beloved,
my Companion,
my Desert Bread,
my Guide upon the Way.

RECOGNITION

WE confess our unfaithfulness:

**our pride,
hypocrisy,
and impatience;**

**our self-indulgent
appetites
and ways;**

**our exploitation
of other people;**

**the violence, envy,
and ruthless greed
in our hearts
and deeds;**

**our idleness
in ease and comfort,
and our possessiveness;**

**our neglect of prayer,
and our failure
to live our faith ...**

GOD of Holiness,
we tremble in your presence.

You show us
how far we have wandered
in a land that is waste,

you face us
with the truth
of our lack of love,

you uncover
the layers
of our illusions,

you pierce us
with the sword
that heals,

you embrace us
with a purging fire,

you refuse
to let us go.

**God of Holiness,
we tremble in your presence.**

PSALMS

ETERNAL Spirit,
flow through our being
and open our lips,
**that our mouths
may proclaim your praise.**

Let us worship
the God of Love:
Alleluia. Alleluia.

OUT of the depths
I have called to you, O God:
O God of compassion,
hear my voice.
**Open your heart to me,
my cry wells within me.
If you keep account of my sins,
I cannot stand.**
But there is forgiveness
with you,
your way
is my life.

**I wait for you, my God,
my soul waits for you.
I wait with my heart,
I hope for your word.**
I look for you
as a watchman
looks for the morning,
more I say
than a watchman
for the morning.
**For you will fulfil
your promise to rescue me,
you will free me
from the grip of evil.**
I put my trust
in you,
**O God of mercy
and compassion.**

WHEN God takes us home
from our exile,
we shall wake from our dream
and live again.
**We shall sing
and laugh for joy;
the whole world
will acclaim God's wonders.**

O God, you will do
great things for us,
and we shall rejoice
and praise your name.
Take us home,
bring us to life,
like rivers in the desert
when the first rains fall.
We go on our way sadly,
with tears
sowing seeds.
We shall return with joy,
with gladness
bearing our sheaves.

READING

THIS is my commandment,
that you love one another,
even as I have loved you.
You can have no greater love than this,
than to lay down your life
for your friends.

ALL you who are led
by the Spirit of God
are children of God ...

For you did not receive
the spirit of fear,
but you have received
the spirit of adoption ...

When we cry,
Abba, Father,
it is the Spirit
bearing witness with our spirit
that we are children of God ...

and if children, then heirs,
heirs of God
and fellow heirs with Christ ...

provided we suffer with him
that we may also
be glorified with him.

WE know
that the whole creation itself
will be set free
from its bondage to decay,
having been groaning in travail
together until now;
and not only the creation,
but we ourselves,
who have the firstfruits
of the Spirit,
groan inwardly
as we wait for our adoption
as sons and daughters,
the redemption of our bodies,
and obtain the glorious liberty
of the children of God.

I AM sure that neither death
nor life, nor angels,
nor principalities nor powers,
nor things present
nor things to come,
nor height nor depth,
nor anything else in all creation
will be able to separate us
from the love of God
in Christ Jesus.

HYMN

O THOU who camest from above,
The fire celestial to impart,
Kindle a flame of sacred love
On the low altar of my heart.

There let it for thy glory burn
With inextinguishable blaze,
And trembling to its source return
In humble prayer and fervent praise.

Jesus confirm my heart's desire
To work and speak and think for thee,
Still let me guard the holy fire,
And still stir up thy gift in me.

Ready for all thy perfect will,
My acts of faith and love repeat,
Till death thine endless mercies seal,
And make the sacrifice complete.

INTO YOUR HANDS

INTO your hands
I commend the whole of my being,
for you have redeemed me,
body and soul,
O God of truth and love.

Keep me, dear God,
as the apple of an eye,
hide me under the shadow
of your wings.

ANTIPHON TO THE NUNC DIMITTIS

PRESERVE us,
dear God,
while waking,
and guard us
while sleeping,
that awake
we may watch
with Christ,
and asleep
we may rest
in your peace.

NUNC DIMITTIS

PRAISE be to God,
I have lived to see this day.
God's promise is fulfilled,
and my duty done.

At last you have given me peace,
for I have seen with my own eyes
the salvation you have prepared
for all nations,
a light to the world
in its darkness,
and the glory
of your people Israel.

Glory be to God,
sustaining, redeeming, sanctifying,
as in the beginning,
so now, and for ever. Amen.

KYRIES

KYRIE eleison
Christe eleison
Kyrie eleison

PRAYING WITH CHRIST

DEAR God,
our Creator,
Beloved Companion
and Guide upon the Way,
Eternal Spirit
within us
and beyond us ...

Let us honour
your name
in lives of costly,
giving love ...

Let us show that we
and all whom we meet
deserve dignity and respect,
for they are your dwelling place
and your home ...

Let us share in action
your deep desire
for justice and peace
among the peoples
of the world ...

Let us share our bread
with one another,
the bread that you have shared
with us ...

Let us in the spirit
of your forgiving us,
make friends
with those we have harmed
and failed to love ...

Let us overcome
our trials and temptations,
our suffering and dying,
in the strength and courage
with which you overcame them too ...

Let us in your love
free the world from evil,
transforming darkness into light ...

For the whole universe is yours,
and you invite us to be partners
in the work of your creating ...

Amen. So be it.
So will we do it.

I WILL LIE DOWN IN PEACE

I WILL lie down in peace
and take my rest,
**for it is in God alone
that I dwell unafraid.**

Let us bless the Life-Giver,
the Pain-Bearer, the Love-Maker;
**let us praise and exalt God
above all for ever.**

May God's name be praised
beyond the furthest star,
**glorified and exalted
above all for ever.**

[PARTICULAR PRAYERS]

CHRIST CRUCIFIED

CHRIST crucified,
nailed to the unyielding wood,
Bearer to us
of the true and living God,

(whose flesh was pecked
by the carrion of the air,
whose bones were gnawed
by the wild dogs,)

give us courage
to face what must decay,
the disintegration
of our mortal flesh,

and give us faith
to shed our false
and deadly selves,
to let them be as smoke
vanishing in the evening breeze,

that as soul-bodies
we may grow
through all our days,
refined to a finer tuning
than we can yet discern,
shaped into the likeness
of your transfigured,
risen body,

that our true
and lively selves,
fresh embodied,
living flames at last,
may dwell and dance with you,
in love, for ever.

LIGHTEN OUR DARKNESS

LIGHTEN our darkness,
we ask of you, dear God,
and in your great mercy
strengthen us to face
all perils and dangers
of the night;
for the love of your only Son,
our Saviour Jesus Christ.

BLESSING

THE blessing of God,
the shalom of God
the wildness
and the warmth of God,
be among us
and between us,
now and always.

The divine Spirit
dwells in us:
Thanks be to God.

SATURDAY

INVOCATION

THE angels of God guard us
through the night,
**and quieten
the powers of darkness.**

The Spirit of God
be our guide
**to lead us to peace
and to glory.**

IT is but lost labour that you haste to rise up early,
and so late take rest, and eat the bread of anxiety.
For those beloved of God are given gifts even while
they sleep.

OUR help is in the name
of the eternal God,
**who is making
the heavens and the earth.**

THANKSGIVING

DEAR God, thank you
for all that is good,
for our creation
and our humanity,
for the stewardship
you have given us
of this planet earth,
for the gifts of life
and of one another,

[for the people and events
of this day]

[for the communion of saints]

for your Love,
unbounded and eternal …

O Thou,
Most Holy and Beloved,
my Companion,
my Counsellor,
my Guide upon the Way.

RECOGNITION

WE repent the wrongs we have done:

**our blindness
to human need and suffering;**

**our indifference
to injustice and cruelty;**

**our false judgments,
petty thoughts,
and contempt;**

**our waste and pollution
of the earth and oceans;**

**our lack of concern
for those who come after us;**

**our complicity
in the making of instruments
of mass destruction,
and our threatening their use ...**

ETERNAL Spirit,
living God,

in whom we live
and move
and have our being,

all that we are,
have been,
and shall be
is known to you,

to the secrets of our hearts
and all that rises
to trouble us.

**Living Flame,
burn into us;**

**Cleansing Wind,
blow through us;**

**Fountain of Water,
well up within us,**

**that we may love and praise
in deed and in truth.**

PSALM

ETERNAL Spirit,
flow through our being
and open our lips,
**that our mouths
may proclaim your praise.**

Let us worship
the God of Love:
Alleluia. Alleluia.

AS a deer longs
for streams of living water,
**so longs my soul
for you, O God.**
My soul is thirsty
for the living God:
**when shall I draw near
to see your face?**
My tears have been my food
in the night:
**all day long they ask me,
Where now is your God?**
As I pour out my soul
in distress,

**I remember how I went
to the temple of God,**
with shouts and songs
of thanksgiving,
**a multitude
keeping high festival.**
Why are you so full
of heaviness, my soul,
**and why so rebellious
within me?**
Put your trust in God,
patiently wait for the dawn,
**and you will then praise
your deliverer and your God.**

My soul is heavy within me;
therefore I remember you
**from the land of Jordan
and from the hills of Hermon.**
Deep calls to deep
in the roar of your waterfalls;
**all your waves and your torrents
have gone over me.**
Surely, O God,
you will show me mercy
in the daytime,

and at night
I will sing your praise,
O God of my life.
I will say to God, my rock,
Why have you forgotten me?
Why must I go like a mourner
because the enemy oppresses me?
Like a sword piercing my bones,
my enemies have mocked me,
asking me all day long,
Where now is your God?
Why are you so full
of heaviness, my soul,
and why so rebellious
within me?
Put your trust in God,
patiently wait for the dawn,
and you will then praise
your deliverer and your God.

O God, take up my cause
and strive for me
with a godless people
that knows no mercy.
Save me from the grip
of cunning and lies,

**for you are my God
and my strength.**
Why have you cast me away
from your presence?
**Why must I be clothed in rags,
humiliated by my enemy?**
O send out your light and your truth,
and let them lead me,
**let them guide me to your holy hill
and to your dwelling.**
Then I shall go to the altar of God,
the God of my joy and delight,
**and to the harp I shall sing your
    praises,
O God my God.**
Why are you so full
of heaviness, my soul,
**and why so rebellious
within me?**
Put your trust in God,
patiently wait for the dawn,
**and you will then praise
your deliverer and your God.**

READING

THERE is great gain
in godliness with contentment.
For we brought nothing
into this world,
and we cannot take anything
out of it.
But if we have food and clothing,
with these we shall be content ...

For the love of money
is the root of all evils ...

So shun all this:
aim at justice, Christlikeness,
fidelity, steadfastness, gentleness ...

OPEN your mouth for the dumb,
for the rights of those
who are left desolate.
Open your mouth,
judge righteously,
maintain the rights of the poor
and the needy ...

THOUGH our outer nature
is wasting away,
our inner nature
is being renewed every day.
For this slight momentary affliction
is preparing us for an eternal weight
of glory beyond comparison,
because we look not to the things
that are seen,
but to the things
that are unseen;
for the things that are seen
are transient,
but the things that are unseen
are eternal …

THE Spirit of God is upon me, anointing me to preach good news to the poor, sending me to proclaim release to the captives and recovering of sight to the blind, to set at liberty those who are oppressed, to proclaim the time of God's grace and favour …

HYMN

BE still in God's Presence,
Be still in God's Presence,
Be still in God's Presence,
   And love and be loved.

Be still in God's Presence,
Be still in God's Presence,
Be still in God's Presence,
   And love and be loved.

Fall deep in the silence,
Fall deep in the silence,
Fall deep in the silence,
   The silence of God,

Fall deep in the silence,
Fall deep in the silence,
Fall deep in the silence,
   The silence of God.

INTO YOUR HANDS

INTO your hands
I commend the whole of my being,
for you have redeemed me,
body and soul,
O God of truth and love.

Keep me, dear God,
as the apple of an eye,
hide me under the shadow
of your wings.

ANTIPHON TO THE NUNC DIMITTIS

PRESERVE us,
dear God,
while waking,
and guard us
while sleeping,
that awake
we may watch
with Christ,
and asleep
we may rest
in your peace.

NUNC DIMITTIS

PRAISE be to God,
I have lived to see this day.
God's promise is fulfilled,
and my duty done.

At last you have given me peace,
for I have seen with my own eyes
the salvation you have prepared
for all nations,
a light to the world
in its darkness,
and the glory
of your people Israel.

Glory be to God,
sustaining, redeeming, sanctifying,
as in the beginning,
so now, and for ever. Amen.

KYRIES

KYRIE eleison
Christe eleison
Kyrie eleison

PRAYING IN CHRIST

Abba, Amma, Beloved ...
your name be hallowed ...
your reign spread among us ...
your will be done well ...
at all times, in all places ...
on earth, as in heaven ...

Give us the bread ...
we need for today ...
Forgive us our trespass ...
as we forgive those ...
who trespass against us ...
Let us not fail ...
in time of our testing ...
Spare us from trials ...
too sharp to endure ...
Free us from the grip ...
of all evil powers ...

For yours is the reign ...
the power and the glory ...
the victory of love ...
for time and eternity ...
world without end ...
So be it. Amen ...

I WILL LIE DOWN IN PEACE

I WILL lie down in peace
and take my rest,
**for it is in God alone
that I dwell unafraid.**

Let us bless the Life-Giver,
the Pain-Bearer, the Love-Maker;
**let us praise and exalt God
above all for ever.**

May God's name be praised
beyond the furthest star,
**glorified and exalted
above all for ever.**

[PARTICULAR PRAYERS]

LOVING GOD

LOVING God,
you have prepared
for those who love you
such good things
as pass our understanding.

Pour into our hearts
such love towards you,
that we may love you
in all things,
and love you
beyond everything,

and so inherit
your promises,
which exceed
all we can desire,

in Jesus Christ,
ever-loving
and ever-beloved.

ABIDING AND INCREASING

INDWELLING God,
strengthen your servants
with your heavenly grace,
that we may continue
yours for ever,
and daily increase
in your Holy Spirit
more and more
until we come to share
in the glory of your Kingdom.

BLESSING

BLESSING, light, and glory
surround us
and scatter the darkness
of the long and lonely night.

The divine Spirit dwells in us:
Thanks be to God.

READINGS AND
ANTIPHONS TO THE
NUNC DIMITTIS

for special days and seasons

ADVENT

Reading

A voice cries,
In the wilderness
prepare the way of Yahweh:
make straight in the desert
a highway for our God.
Every valley shall be lifted up,
and every mountain and hill made low:
the uneven ground shall become level,
and the rough places a plain.
And the glory of Yahweh shall be
    revealed,
and all flesh shall see it together.

Antiphon

Come, O God,
and visit us in peace,
that we may rejoice
in your presence
with a perfect heart.

CHRISTMAS

Reading

The Word became flesh
and dwelt among us.
We beheld the glory of God
shining through a human face –
as a mother's eyes
live through her daughter's,
and as a son reflects
his father's image –
the glory of God
in a human being fully alive.

Antiphon

Alleluia.
The Word was made flesh,
Alleluia,
and dwelt among us,
Alleluia, Alleluia.

EPIPHANY

Reading

Our eyes have seen your salvation,
which you have prepared for all peoples,
a light to enlighten the nations,
and give glory to your people Israel.

Antiphon

Alleluia.
All nations shall come
before God,
Alleluia,
and they will glorify
God's holy name,
Alleluia, Alleluia.

LENT

Reading

Is not this the fast that I choose:
to loose the bonds of wickedness,
to undo the thong of the yoke,
to let the oppressed go free,
and to break every prison bar?
Is it not to share your bread with the hungry,
and to bring the homeless poor into your house,
when you see the naked, to cover him,
and not to hide yourself from your own flesh?
Then shall your light break forth as the dawn,
and your healing shall spring up speedily.

Antiphon

For their sake
I consecrate myself,
that they also
may be consecrated in truth.

PASSIONTIDE

Reading

He was scourged for our faults,
he was bruised for our sins.
On him lies the chastisement
that makes us whole,
and with his wounds
we are healed.

Antiphon

Christ became obedient
to death,
even death on a cross.

EASTER

Reading

Christ is risen from the dead,
and become the firstfruits
of those who slept.
As death came into the world
by a human being,
so also has come
the resurrection of the dead.
For as in Adam all die,
even so in Christ
shall all be made alive.

Antiphon

Alleluia.
Christ is risen,
Alleluia.
He is risen indeed,
Alleluia, alleluia.

ASCENSION

Reading

Christ reigns,
disarming
the principalities and powers,
triumphing
over evil and pain and death.
Christ is with us always,
to the end of time.

Antiphon

Alleluia.
The pioneer of our salvation
has triumphed over suffering
    and death,
Alleluia.
The firstborn among many
    sisters and brothers
has led the way into the presence
    of God,
Alleluia, alleluia.

PENTECOST

Reading

The love of God
has been shed abroad
in our hearts
through the Holy Spirit
who has been given to us.

For God has not given us
a spirit of fear,
but of power
and of love
and of a sound mind.

Antiphon

Alleluia.
The Holy Spirit
will teach you all things,
Alleluia,
and will guide you
into all truth,
Alleluia, Alleluia.

TRINITY

Reading

Countless angels praise you
and sing to you
with ceaseless voice:
Holy, holy, holy is God,
who was and who is
and who is to come, Amen.
Blessing and glory
and wisdom and thanksgiving
and power and love
be to our God for ever and ever.

Antiphon

Alleluia.
Great praise
and everlasting glory
be to God,
Lover, Beloved, Mutual Friend,
Alleluia,
Life-giver, Pain-bearer,
    Love-maker,
Alleluia, Alleluia.

SAINTS' DAYS

Reading

These are the words of the First and the Last, who was dead and came to life again: To those who are victorious I will give the right to eat from the tree of life that stands in the Garden of God, alleluia. Be faithful to death, and I will give you the crown of life, alleluia. To those who are victorious I will give some of the hidden manna. I will give them also a white stone, alleluia. And on the stone will be written a new name, known only to the one who receives it, alleluia.

Antiphon

Alleluia.
The Lamb who was slain
has conquered,
alleluia.
All who follow the Way
will share in the victory,
alleluia, alleluia.

THE DEPARTED

Reading

Thanks be to God, because in Christ's victory over the grave, a new age has dawned, the reign of sin is over, a broken world is being renewed, and we are once again made whole. As we believe that Jesus died and rose again, so we believe it will be for those who have died: God will bring them to life with Christ Jesus.

Antiphon

Give rest, O Christ,
to your servant(s)
with your saints,
where sorrow and pain
are no more,
neither sighing,
but life everlasting.

PARTICULAR PRAYERS

SUNDAY

MONDAY

TUESDAY

WEDNESDAY

THURSDAY

FRIDAY

SATURDAY

ADDITIONAL PRAYERS

GOD BLESS ...

God bless this city
and move our hearts with pity
lest we grow hard ...

God bless this house
with silence, solitude, simplicity
that we may pray ...

God bless these days
of rough and narrow ways
lest we despair ...

God bless the night
and calm the people's fright
that we may love ...

God bless this land
and guide us with your hand
lest we be unjust ...

God bless this earth
through pangs of death and birth
and make us whole ...

GOD BE ...

God be in my head
and in my understanding ...
God be in my eyes
and in my looking ...
God be in my mouth
and in my speaking ...
God be in my tongue
and in my tasting ...
God be in my lips
and in my greeting ...

God be in my nose
and in my scenting ...
God be in my ears
and in my hearing ...
God be in my neck
and in my humbling ...
God be in my shoulders
and in my bearing ...
God be in my back
and in my standing ...

God be in my arms
and in my reaching …
God be in my hands
and in my working …
God be in my legs
and in my walking …
God be in my feet
and in my grounding …
God be in my joints
and in my relating …

God be in my guts
and in my feeling …
God be in my bowels
and in my forgiving …
God be in my loins
and in my swiving …
God be in my lungs
and in my breathing …
God be in my heart
and in my loving …

God be in my skin
and in my touching ...
God be in my flesh
and in my yearning ...
God be in my blood
and in my living ...
God be in my bones
and in my dying ...
God be at my end
and at my beginning ...

TO THE TROUBLING UNKNOWN

The fauna of the night,
hidden in the grass
of your neglect …

Encounter them …
Contemplate them …
Dare to look steadily at them …
Wrestle with them …
Expect to be wounded
in the struggle with them …
Name them …
Recognize them …
And be blessed by them …

At the breaking of dawn
they will be known
as delectable creatures,
no longer exiled,
but returned to you,
made precious again,
moving with you
into the future,
robed as destinies …

To the powers of dis-ease
within us
and among us
and through the world,
troubling us,
entangling us,
distracting us,
wounding us,
holding us in their grip …

Whatever be your name,
greed, pride, malice, envy, evil,
grief, rage, fear, pain, death …

known in the secret places
of our hearts,
or as yet unknown to us,
or greater in strength
than any one of us
can bear alone,
come out of darkness
into light,
into the Presence of the
Pain-Bearing,
Love-Making,
Life-Giving
God …

that we may understand
and withstand you …

that we may know
your name and nature …

that you may ease
your hold upon us …

that you may wound us
no more …

that you may be transformed
by the power of that Love
which is deeper
than the deepest pain,
so yielding your energy
in the service of God,
freeing us together
to be the friends of God,
and to live
to reflect God's glory …

And where,
through lack of prayer
or fasting,

through weak will
or faint heart,

through the mysteries
of the unresolved,

through fear
of your power to destroy,

we cannot yet be reconciled,

leave us be,
depart and trouble us not tonight,
and wait awhile constrained,

until together we can face
the refining, warming,
life-enhancing flame
of the judging,
healing, loving God …

You are troubled
by your dark angels ...

You seek to tame
their wildness ...

But they are the source
of creativity within you ...

If you deny them,
banish them,
seek to destroy them,
they will drain you of passion
as they retreat,
and you will become
pale and lifeless ...

And if they should return
and storm your gates,
you would be then
sore wounded ...

However dark,
they are still angels,
guardians and protectors too ...

IN THE LIFE OF THE CITY AT NIGHT

the Spirit is suffering, striving, creating

Blessings,
guidance,
and fierce
and tender love
for those who wake
while others sleep:

on night shifts in factories …

watching over buildings …

travelling through the city …

cleaning offices …

stocking supermarket shelves …

in ambulances, police cars,
fire engines …

observing and researching …

alert at power stations and
waterworks

at telephone exchanges …

at parties and night clubs …

driving taxis, buses, coaches,
trains …

flying over the city in planes …

speeding by the city on
motorways …

thieving and attacking in the
dark …

searching out the secrets of
others …

hustling and walking the
streets …

huddling in doorways …

listening to those in despair …

crying out in loneliness …

suddenly taken ill ...

trying to sleep but cannot ...

restless and awake in hospital ...

coping with crises ...

watching and caring ...

awake with young children ...

calming the confused ...

dying at home, in hospice or
hospital ...

keeping vigil with them ...

... and those on the other side of
the world for whom it is day ...

A PRAYER OF SURRENDER

Abba, Amma, Beloved,
I abandon myself
into your hands …

In your love for me
do as you will …

Whatever that may prove to be
I am thankful …

I am ready for all,
I accept all …

Let only your will
be done in me,
as in all your creatures,
and I will ask nothing else …

Into your hands
I commend my whole being …

I give you myself
with the love of my heart …

For I love you, my God,
and so I need to give …

to surrender myself
into your hands …

with a trust
beyond measure …

For you are
my faithful Creator …

Abba …

Amma …

Beloved …

Friend …

GOD'S COVENANT WITH ME/US

I Who Am and Who Shall Be,
Love-Making Spirit within you,
Pain-Bearing Presence beside you,
Life-Giving Future before you,

I call you into being
and bind myself to you.

By my own name and nature,
in every eternal moment,

I affirm and renew my covenant,
I fulfil my deepest promise,

to love you to glory for ever,
to honour you as my home,
and to be loyal to you
and full of faith in you,
our life-day long.

Amen. So be it.

MY/OUR COVENANT WITH GOD

Beloved and faithful Creator,

Love-Making Spirit within me,
Pain-Bearing Presence beside me,
Life-Giving Future before me,

of my own free will
I choose to share my life with you.
This day and all my days
I affirm and renew my covenant,
I fulfil my deepest promise,

to love you in friendship for ever,
to honour you as my home,
and to be loyal to you
and full of faith in you,
our life-day long.

Amen. So be it.

A COVENANT OF FRIENDSHIP

In the wonderful Mystery of God,

Love-Making Spirit between us,
Pain-Bearing Presence beside us,
Life-Giving Future before us,

you have been given to me,
to be cherished in friendship.

By my own free will and destiny
I choose to share my life with you.

With and in that greater Love
I promise to do all that I can
for your well-being for ever,

to honour you as God's home,
and to be loyal to you
and full of faith in you,
our life-day long.

Amen. So be it.

FOR FRIENDS, HERE AND BEYOND

God of the living,
in whose embrace
all creatures live,
in whatever world
or condition they may be,
I remember in prayer
those whose names and needs
and dwelling place
are known to you ...

giving you thanks for them,
and for my memories of them ...

In you, dear God,
I love them.
May these waves
of prayerful love
minister to their peace
and to their growth in grace ...

I pray in and through Jesus Christ,
who broke the barrier
of time and space and death
and is alive for ever.